Copyright © 2021 by Lara Jean

All rights reserved. This book or any portion thereof may not be reproduced or used in any manner whatsoever without the express written permission of the publisher except for the use of brief quotations in a book review.

This work is sold with the understanding that neither the author nor the publisher are held responsible for the results accrued from the advice in this book. All plants, animals, and insects in this book should be treated with caution.

Printed in the United States of America

First Printing, July 2020

ISBN 978-1-7352791-1-4

Lara Jean Doodles

www.larajeandoodles.weebly.com

larajeandoodles@gmail.com

BE KIND TO ME

a book of reasons to love
the important
underappreciated things

by Lara Jean

Our planet is a fascinatingly diverse and wonderfully unique place, full of all kinds of creatures and plants.

Each is important in its own way, and although some may seem strange or frightening or even inconvenient for us, it is important to remember the value of each creature and plant.

This book introduces just a few of these often unloved things, and reminds us why they are important, and why it is so vital to be kind.

I am a little seedling. Though I don't look like much now, one day I'll be bigger than you—even bigger than your house—reaching for the sky! When I'm a fully grown tree, you can sit under me for a picnic, climb up into my branches to read a book, and hang feeders from my boughs for birds. I'll provide shade, safe homes for animals, nuts and leaves to eat, and I'll even produce the oxygen you need to breathe! So please, be kind to me.

I am a dandelion. I pop up everywhere—in your lawn, in your garden, in the sidewalk cracks... I'm not picky! In the spring I'm eager to bloom, and you'll see my sunny yellow flowers until the very last days of autumn. When the bees wake up in the spring, I'm ready to offer them food. If you pull me up or spray me with chemicals, I can't be there to be safe food for the bees. So please, be kind to me.

We are wild flowers, aren't we pretty? We are native plants; this is our home. All the animals and bugs know us and depend on us for food. They know what parts of us are safe to eat and where we are to be found. If you mow us down or pick all of us, we can't mingle and produce seeds so we can grow year after year. If you spray us with chemicals, we become unsafe to eat. Consider planting us instead of treating us like weeds. We are necessary for the wildlife you love. So please, be kind to us.

We are a grub and a worm. We are wonderfully squirmy, slimy, unique-looking creatures. If you see a worm in the dirt, you should be very excited because we make healthy soil. It's our job to tunnel through the ground and help loosen up the soil for young plants. We also play valuable roles at the bottom of the food chain, and we are often snacks for all kinds of creatures, including birds and bears! You can't have beautiful gardens with lush flowers without us to make the soil healthy. So please, be kind to us.

I am a honey bee. Yes, I can sting. But only when I've been scared by your screaming, waving, swatting, and stamping! Most of the time, I just fly from flower to flower, sipping on sugary nectar and carrying pollen on to the next plant. This pollinates flowers so plants can grow seeds and delicious fruits! I also make honey—and plenty of it—so you can enjoy a tasty treat on your toast or in your tea. I need all kinds of flowers for my food, from the dandelion to the bell pepper flower to the rose. Please don't spray my food with poisonous insecticides! All I want to do is peacefully pollinate. So please, be kind to me.

I am a wasp. Though I look different, I'm actually a lot like the honey bee. I pollinate flowers, but that's not all! I'm also a hunter, and I catch those bugs you really can't stand—mosquitoes! Pest insects that can destroy plants are my ideal meal. Just like the honey bee, I'll mind my own business if you let me be. Though I'll defend my home fiercely, I'd much rather focus on hunting than stinging you. I like to be left alone, and in return I'll keep those pesky mosquitoes and aphids under control. So please, be kind to me.

I am a spider. Don't be afraid! I'm not interested in you at all; I don't want to get into your hair or your clothes. I just want to make my elegant silken home and enjoy some peace and quiet. Like a wasp, I'm an important hunter responsible for pest control in your garden. I eat as many mosquitoes and gnats as I can catch! If you find me in your home, please just put me back outside. I want to be out hunting, not squashed just because you think I look scary! So please, be kind to me.

I am a moth. Moths can come in all shapes and sizes, and are often out at both night and day. I'd bet that you have mistaken some of us, like the yellow cabbage moth or the elegant green luna moth, for butterflies! Just like a butterfly, I'm a pollinator. Some flowers bloom only at night just for me! Unfortunately, I can be very confused by outdoor lights left on all night. I need it to be dark, really dark, so that I don't get distracted. Please turn your lights off so I can find my food! I can't sting or bite, so don't be afraid of me. I just flutter about and pollinate! So please, be kind to me.

I am a bat. I have wonderfully leathery wings that stretch between my fingers, and I fly about at night. Don't be afraid—I'm not a vampire! I'm not interested in you at all. I can see perfectly in the dark, thanks to my excellent hearing. My favorite things to eat are bugs! In some places, I also pollinate plants. Please consider making me a bat house so I have a place to sleep—that way I won't be tempted by your attic. Having me around to eat the mosquitoes is really handy! So please, be kind to me.

I am a mouse. And believe me, I'm much more afraid of you than you are of me! I'm shy and hungry. My job is to find all the little seeds and bugs to eat. I manage overgrowth by using grass for my nests, I eat grubs and beetles so they don't take over, and I spread seeds to help plants grow! If I've snuck into your home, it's best to trap me and release me to a field—I've got lots of seeds to harvest! Please don't poison me. I'm often a snack for owls and cats, and if I've eaten poison I'll poison them, too. So please, be kind to me.

I am a squirrel. You probably see me all over the place. I can be a little silly, and if I dash across the road, you might not feel like slowing down for me in your big fast car. But I've got babies at home, and they need me to find food for them! My favorite foods are nuts and seeds, which I stash in the ground for safekeeping. Often I don't come back for all of them, and those seeds I leave behind turn into huge, healthy trees. I can plant so many trees that whole forests grow just from my work. So please, be kind to me.

I am an opossum. In North America, there's nobody else like me! I'm a marsupial, which means I carry my babies in a pouch on my belly, like a kangaroo. You are probably an omnivore, which means you eat all kinds of foods. I'm an omnivore, too. I don't let anything go to waste. At night, I search for snacks, and one of my favorites is ticks! I can't get Lyme disease, so I'm protecting you from these nasty little bugs. If you come across me, I might play dead so that you'll leave me alone. Please don't be scared by my sharp teeth or my pink prehensile tail. I'm just cleaning up! So please, be kind to me.

I am a vulture. Much like the opossum, I'm often disliked for my unusual appearance. But I'm so very important! My head is bald so that it stays clean while I'm doing my job, which is to clean! I make sure nothing goes to waste, and I tidy up any messes left laying around. Without me, there would be tons of stinky unpleasantness left all over. I'm big and not fast at taking flight, so you need to keep an eye out for me on roadsides. That's where there's the most work to be done! So please, be kind to me.

I am leaf litter. Don't let the word litter fool you; I'm not trash. In fact, without me there's no dirt for plants to grow in. I'm both a home and food for the grubs and worms! Mushrooms need leaf litter and rotting logs to grow, and mushrooms are food for animals, as well as aids to the process of turning me into soil. Don't bag me up, especially not in plastic. Please let me rest and decompose. If I'm all over your lawn, just mow me in so I can still do my job. I'm vital to the ecosystem. So please, be kind to me.

Ways you can be kind to our planet and its creatures:

1. Use canvas shopping bags

2. Recycle

3. Reduce the amount of plastic packaging you buy, use tab toothpaste, bar soap, and shop at bulk food stores so you can reuse your own bags

4. Don't buy bottled water; use a glass or metal bottle instead

5. Participate in highway, beach, and river cleanups

6. Plant bee-friendly local wildflowers

7. Don't use chemical weed killers on your lawn or garden

8. Build bee houses and bat houses

9. Turn lights off at night, as well as electronics, to reduce electricity use

10. Research! Use the internet to find resources about things you can do to help. There are so many ways to be kind!

Thank You:

To all my friends and family who have been here for me as I've stumbled along on this journey! And to you, reader, for taking the time to learn about these creatures. THANK YOU for being so kind.

Lara is an artist from Michigan. She illustrates, writes, gardens, and is a lover of all the creepy-crawlers and wild plants.

You can find her work online:

www.etsy.com/shop/larajeandoodles

www.larajeandoodles.weebly.com

You can also follow her on social media @larajeandoodles

CPSIA information can be obtained
at www.ICGtesting.com
Printed in the USA
LVHW051523301021
701631LV00002B/23